The Battle of Point Pleasant

A Critical Event at the Onset of a Revolution

Colin Mustful

The Battle of Point Pleasant: A Critical Event at the Onset of a Revolution

ISBN: 978-1-300-16424-1

Contents

Abstract

Just six months prior to the onset of the American Revolution a major battle raged between colonial Virginians and the native Indians of western Virginia. This was the Battle of Point Pleasant fought on October 10, 1774. For various reasons, this battle has been recognized by some as the first battle of the American Revolution. However, evidence clearly shows that the Battle of Point Pleasant had no connection with the American Revolution. Rather, the Battle of Point Pleasant was the final battle of the American Colonial Wars. Though it was not a part of the Revolution, it was a critical event in American history that acted to open the settlement of the west and to free Colonial resources to ensure victory in the war for independence.

On October 10, 1774, the principle event of Lord Dunmore's War, the Battle of Point Pleasant, raged between colonial Virginians and the native Indians of western Virginia. The battle ended in just one day with the retreat of the natives and victory for the settlers. The Battle of Point Pleasant resulted in the subjugation of western Indian tribes and in the advancement of the line of settlement west from the Alleghany Mountains to the Ohio River. Furthermore, victory for the colonial Virginians quieted tensions between Indians and settlers which allowed all necessary resources to be employed toward the approaching Revolutionary War against the British.

The Battle of Point Pleasant was a significant and consequential event in the history of the United States, however, its place in that history is controversial. Accusations made against John Murray the Earl of Dunmore, the governor of Virginia, suggest that he incited the battle in order to weaken the citizen militia of Virginia giving the British a greater advantage over colonial powers. Also, some argue that the Indians colluded with Dunmore and were therefore allied with the British as early as 1774. These arguments propose that the Battle of Point Pleasant should be recognized as the first battle of the American Revolution. However, existing evidence from and prior to the Battle of Point Pleasant show otherwise. Firstly, the Battle of Point Pleasant was the conclusion to a series of colonial conflicts. Secondly, Lord Dunmore was loyal to the Virginians and their cause. Finally, the Indians were in no way allied with the British until several years following the Battle of Point Pleasant. Therefore, the Battle of Point Pleasant was fought solely over previous depredations between settlers and Indians and over rights to frontier lands and should be marked as the final battle of the American Colonial Wars.

The Battle of Point Pleasant was the result of years of conflict which began many years before the event occurred. The most notable starting point for the battle came in a proclamation by Colonel Henry Bouquet at Fort Pitt in 1758.[1] In his proclamation Colonel Bouquet established the westward line of settlement at the Alleghany Mountains thereby forbidding the citizens of Virginia to settle or hunt west of this line, leaving it solely to the Indians.[2] The proclamation, however, was largely ignored. Colonial Virginians had an ardent desire to continue settlement on new lands regardless of risk or government decree.[3] Lord Dunmore summarized this attitude in his official report of the battle:

---

[1] For the content of the 1758 Proclamation refer to appendix C.

[2] Wills De Hass, *History of the Early Settlement and Indian Wars of Western Virginia* (Wheeling, WV: H.Hoblitzell, 1851), 131.

[3] In his book, *The Winning of the West*, Theodore Roosevelt showed considerable appreciation for the settler's adventuress attitude. Regarding the settlers he wrote, "the West was neither discovered, won, nor settled by any single man. No keen-eyed statesman planned the movement, nor was it carried out by any great military leader; it was the work of a whole people, of whom each man was impelled mainly by sheer love of adventure; it was the outcome of the ceaseless strivings of all the dauntless, restless backwoods folk to win homes for their descendants and to each penetrate deeper than his neighbors into the remote forest hunting-grounds where the perilous pleasures of the

> I have learnt from experience that the established authority of any government in America, and the policy of government at home, are both insufficient to restrain the Americans; and that they do and will remove as their avidity and restlessness incite them. They acquire no attachment to place: but wandering seems engrafted in their nature; and it is a weakness incident to it, that they should for ever imagine the lands further off, are still better than those upon which they are already settled.[4]

Following the 1758 proclamation, conflict grew as settlers pushed toward the Ohio River. Attempts to protect their land seemed useless as the Indians "felt and expressed both fear and hatred of the influence which surrounded and oppressed him."[5]

---

chase and of war could be best enjoyed. We owe the conquest of the West to all the backwoodsmen, not to any solitary individual among them; where all alike were strong and daring there was no chance for any single man to rise to unquestioned pre-eminence."; Theodore Roosevelt, *The Works of Theodore Roosevelt*, vol. 1, *The Winning of the West* (St. Clair Shores, MI: Scholarly Press, 1977, 1900), 170-171.

[4] Reuben Gold Thwaites and Louise Phelps Kellogg, eds., *Documentary History of Dunmore's War, 1774* (Madison, WI: Wisconsin Historical Society, 1905), 371.

[5] Hass, *History of the Early Settlement*, 135.

Due to growing discord between Indians and settlers over western lands a new agreement was established at Fort Stanwix in 1768. The agreement included the purchase of the land west of the Allegheny Mountains to the Ohio River by the colonial governments of Virginia, Pennsylvania, and New Jersey. Indian representatives from the Iroquois Indians, the Delawares, and the Shawnees were present at Fort Stanwix for the signing of the treaty. However, "the Ohio Indians had no voice in the matter."[6] Furthermore, although the Iroquois signed for themselves and their allies, the Delaware and Shawnee did not sign the treaty. Therefore, while the Iroquois Indians gave up rights to their lands in western Virginia, the Delaware and Shawnee did not. This produced further conflict and mutual wrong-doing, ultimately leading to war.[7] Instead of relenting, the Indians

---

[6] Ibid., 139.

[7] Upon commenting on the Treaty of Fort Stanwix historian Wills De Hass wrote, "it was a better foundation, perhaps, than that

valiantly defended their homes from white encroachment. According to Theodore Roosevelt, "year by year the exasperation of the borderers grew greater and the tale of the wrongs they had to avenge longer."[8]

The next major development in the deadly conflict occurred April 30, 1774, at Yellow Creek.[9] On that day, ten Indians had camped on one side of the creek, while several whites, led by Daniel Greathouse, camped on the other.[10] After inviting the Indians to drink, they were massacred by the whites.[11] Ten in all were slain, several of

---

given by previous treaties, but was essentially worthless; for the lands conveyed were not occupied or hunted on by those conveying them."; Hass, *History of the Early Settlement*, 139.

[8] Theodore Roosevelt, *The Works of Theodore Roosevelt*, vol. 1, *The Winning of the West* (St. Clair Shores, MI: Scholarly Press, 1977, 1900), 229.

[9] Yellow Creek is an affluent of the Ohio River on the Ohio side, approximately fifty miles south from Pittsburgh.

[10] Virgil A. Lewis, *History of the Battle of Point Pleasant* (Charleston, WV: The Tribune Printing Company, 1909), 16-17.

[11] In 1849 Judge Henry Jolly, who was sixteen at the time of the Yellow Creek incident, reminisced the event. In a letter he wrote the following: "In the Spring of the year 1774 a party of Indians encamped on the Northwest of the Ohio, near the mouth of Yellow

which were akin to the Mingo Indian's Chief Logan including Logan's father, brother, and sister.

Although tensions were already high, the Yellow Creek incident catapulted the conflict to perilous levels as the Indians sought retribution. In a letter by Henry Jolly he wrote, "it was the belief of the inhabitants who were capable of reasoning on the subject, that all the depredations committed on the frontiers was by Logan and his party, as a retaliation for the murder of Logan's friends at Yellow Creek."[12] This is supported by Logan himself who vowed to raise his hatchet and take ten for one.[13]

Creek a party of whites called Greathouse's party, lay on the opposite side of the river, the Indians came over to the white party – I think five men, one woman and an infant babe, the whites gave them rum, which three of them drank, and in a short time became very drunk. The other two men and the woman refused, the Sober Indians were challenged to shoot at a mark, to which they agreed, and soon as the[y] emptied their guns, the whites shot them down, the woman attempted to escape by flight, but was also shot down, she lived long enough however to beg mercy for her babe, telling them that it was a kin to themselves, they had a man in the cabin, prepared with a tomahawk for the purpose of killing the three drunk Indians, which was immediately done."; Thwaites, *Documentary History*, 10-11.

[12] Thwaites, *Documentary History*, 14.

[13] Ibid., 13.

Logan was true to his vow and noted after the Battle of Point Pleasant that the Yellow Creek massacre called on him for revenge to which he stated, "I have sought it."[14]

Hatred deepened between both races immediately following the massacre at Yellow Creek and depredations increased. Conflict heightened to the point that no one was removed from danger as each incident led to further incidents. According to historian Virgil A. Lewis, "there was terror along the whole western frontier. Indian atrocities were committed almost daily."[15] Only a few days following the Yellow Creek massacre the settlers of the region began to evacuate. In a letter dated May 8, Colonel William Crawford, who resided in western Virginia at the time, wrote to General George Washington that "our inhabitants are much alarmed, many hundreds having gone over the mountain, and the whole country evacuated as far

---

[14] Roosevelt, *Winning of the West*, 288.

[15] Lewis, *Battle of Point Pleasant*, 17.

as the Monongahela . . . In short, a war is every moment expected."[16] On June 8, just one month later, Crawford wrote again to Washington expressing his fear of the situation by noting, "if something is not done, I am much afraid the whole country must fall into the hands of the enemy . . . I believe an Indian war is unavoidable."[17] Tensions continued and by July 1, in letter to Colonel William Preston, Major Arthur Campbell wrote, "the hour that I so much dreaded is now I am apprehensive near at hand."[18] On August 15, Colonel Preston wrote to General Washington that, "we are greatly harassed by the enemy in this country."[19] The violent events of the frontier led many to believe that war had become the only alternative.

---

[16] C.W. Butterfield, ed., *The Washington-Crawford Letters: Being the Correspondence Between George Washington and William Crawford, from 1767-1781 Concerning Western Lands* (Cincinnati: Robert Clarke & Co., 1877), 48; see appendix A.

[17] Ibid., 51; see appendix A.

[18] Thwaites, *Documentary History*, 57-58; see appendix A.

[19] Ibid., 151.; see appendix A.

On May 5, 1774, just a few days following the Yellow Creek massacre, the House of Burgesses authorized Governor Dunmore to prosecute war against the Indians. Shortly thereafter, Dunmore began war preparations. On June 10, 1774, Lord Dunmore issued a circular letter asking the western counties to organize a militia prepared for aggressive measures.[20] From this order, approximately "five weeks were spent in enlisting, securing provisions, and marching to the appointed rendezvous."[21] The men who enlisted were mere settlers rather than soldiers, but they were willing to fight. In a letter from William Crawford to John Penn, Crawford stated that "the militia is composed of men without character and without fortune."[22]

Once provisions had been made Lord Dunmore left Williamsburg for the frontier in July with several hundred

---

[20] Ibid., xv.

[21] Ibid., xviii.

[22] Butterfield, *The Washington-Crawford Letters*, 43; see appendix A.

men. Then, on July 24, Dunmore ordered Lieutenant Andrew Lewis to go with his men to the mouth of the Kanawha River and ordered that he destroy all Indian villages on his way.[23] At the same time, Dunmore ordered Major Angus McDonald to send an attacking force to the Indian towns in order to delay and divert the Indian forces. On July 26, McDonald proceeded from Fort Fincastle to the Shawnee town of Wappatomica with a force of four hundred men. McDonald encountered minimal Indian resistance and found Wappatomica and other Indian towns to be abandon. Five Indian chiefs were taken hostage, but two succeeded to escape. From this, McDonald and his force burned five Indian villages and cut down seventy acres of corn.[24] The results of the expedition, however,

---

[23] Thwaites, *Documentary History*, xvii.

[24] Ibid., 155-156; For more on McDonald's Expedition see appendix B.

were slight, with "ravages upon the frontiers thereafter increasing rather than diminishing."[25]

Meanwhile, Lord Dunmore had arrived at Fort Dunmore in present day Pittsburgh on September 30, 1774. Dunmore then proceeded to Fort Gower at the mouth of the Hockhocking River, which lay thirteen miles south of Parkersburg. At Fort Gower he met with several other forces on October 9, 1774.[26] His Northern Division totaled 1300 men. General Andrew Lewis, who led the Southern Division of about 1100 men,[27] left westward from Camp Union on September 1, 1774.[28] Lewis proceeded to the mouth of the Kanawha River at Point Pleasant where he arrived on October 1.[29] From there Lewis intended to meet

---

[25] Ibid., 156.

[26] Lewis, *Battle of Point Pleasant*, 40.

[27] Samuel G. Drake, *Biography and History of the Indians of North America from its First Discovery*, 11th ed., (Boston: Benjamin B. Mussey and Co., 1851), 539.

[28] Lewis, *Battle of Point Pleasant*, 30.

with Dunmore's Northern Division at the Pickaway Plains. However, to prevent colonial forces from uniting, Chief Cornstalk of the Shawnees decided to strike.

On the evening of October 9, 1774, Chief Cornstalk and his force of approximately one thousand warriors lay just across the Ohio River. That night, Cornstalk and his men ferried across the Ohio about eight miles north of the fork where General Andrew Lewis and his men were camped.[30] Chief Cornstalk planned to fall upon Lewis' camp early that day. However, on the morning of October 10, two of Lewis' men spotted the large force of Shawnee Indians while out hunting. One was killed, the other returned immediately to camp and declared that he had seen "five acres of ground covered with Indians as thick as they could stand."[31] General Lewis proceeded to send his front division, headed by Charles Lewis, to meet the

---

[29] Drake, *Indians of North America*, 539.

[30] Roosevelt, *Winning of the West*, 276.

[31] Ibid., 277.

Indians, followed by his second division headed by William Fleming.[32]

The two forces collided and the battle was ferocious. Neither side gained or lost ground for several hours. Described by Theodore Roosevelt, "the fight was a succession of single combats, each man sheltering himself behind a stump, or a rock, or tree trunk, the superiority of the backwoodsmen in the use of the rifle being offset by the superiority of their foes in the art of hiding and of shielding themselves from harm."[33] By noon the Indian forces began to weaken, and by one in the afternoon they slowly began to retreat. The battle continued for several more hours, but with far less intensity. The Indians fought valiantly throughout, but could not overcome the settlers. Colonel

---

[32] General Lewis was not involved in direct combat with the Shawnees, however, he received strong praise from William Fleming who wrote, "Col. Lewis . . . behaved with the greatest conduct and prudence and by timely and opportunely supporting the lines secured under God both the victory and prevented the enemy's attempts to break into camp."; Thwaites, *Documentary History*, 253-254.

[33] Roosevelt, *Winning of the West*, 279-280.

William Christian exclaimed that "from what I can gather here I cannot describe the bravery of the enemy in battle."[34] Despite their courage, the Shawnee had to fall back. By four o'clock the Indians shot only to prevent pursuit, and by nightfall they had slipped away across the Ohio River.[35]

Though both sides experienced great loss, the Virginians held ground and earned victory. It is difficult to determine exact losses because the Indians carried off many of their dead, while they threw many others into the river so that their bodies could not be taken and scalped by the frontiersmen. Lieutenant Isaac Shelby noted that "it is beyond doubt their loss in number, far exceeds ours, which is considerable."[36] Indian losses have been approximated

---

[34] Thwaites, *Documentary History*, 264.

[35] Lewis, *The Battle of Point Pleasant*, 47; Historian Wills De Hass commented that, "the gradual retreat of the Indians was one of the most masterly things of the kind ever undertaken in the west."; Hass, *History of the Early Settlement*, 158.

[36] Lewis, *Battle of Point Pleasant*, 45; Isaac Shelby's account of the battle written October 16, 1774; see appendix A.

at two hundred thirty three[37] while the Virginians suffered a loss of seventy five killed and one hundred forty wounded.[38] October 10, 1774 proved successful for settlers of western Virginia, where, as stated by Theodore Roosevelt, "in all the contests waged against the Northwestern Indians during the last half of the eighteenth century there was no other where the whites inflicted so great a relative loss on their foes."[39]

After they safely completed their retreat the Shawnee were left with few options. The Indians were weary and their spirits were broken by defeat. They chose to make peace. On October 17, Lord Dunmore met with Chief Cornstalk and other Indian chieftains at Camp

---

[37] Ibid., 51.

[38] Roosevelt, *Winning of the West*, 282.

[39] Ibid., 291; In a primary account of the battle Major William Fleming wrote, "I believe the Indians never had such a scourging from the English before. They scalped many of their own dead to prevent their falling into our hands, buried numbers, threw many into the Ohio and no doubt carried off many wounded."; Thwaites, *Documentary History*, 256.

Charlotte on the Pickaway Plains in order to write terms of reconciliation. The terms met declared that the Indians would never again "hunt or visit the south side of the Ohio River" in addition to several other stipulations.[40] The treaty was supremely advantageous to the settlers who finally forced the line of settlement permanently west from the Alleghany Mountains to the Ohio River. This advancement allowed for the settlement of western lands including the territory of Kentucky. Commenting on the results of the battle, William Crawford wrote, "I think we may with propriety say we have had great success; as we have made them sensible of their villainy and weakness, and, I hope, made peace with them on such a footing as will be lasting."[41] More importantly, however, victory at Point

---

[40] Lewis, *Battle of Point Pleasant*, 56; For the terms of the Camp Charlotte treaty see appendix C.

[41] Butterfield, *The Washington-Crawford Letters*, 54; Lord Dunmore expressed the opinion that victory at Point Pleasant "has impressed the idea of the power of the white people, upon the minds of the Indians, which they did not before entertain; and, there is reason to

Pleasant allowed soldiers to be free from frontier harassment in order that they could fight the British in the American Revolution.

With the conclusion of the Battle of Point Pleasant the colonial stage ended while the revolutionary stage began. It is contended, however, that the Battle of Point Pleasant did not mark the end of the great colonial period in American history, but rather the beginning of the American Revolution. In 1901, the Battle of Point Pleasant was publicly declared as the first battle of the American Revolution.

The leading argument for the Battle of Point Pleasant as the first battle of the American Revolution was advocated by a Point Pleasant newspaper editor and publisher in the early twentieth century named Livia Simpson-Poffenbarger. Poffenbarger, also a member of the Daughters of the American Revolution, strongly believed

---

believe, it has extinguished the rancor which raged so violently in our people against the Indians."; Thwaites, *Documentary History*, 386.

that Governor Dunmore facilitated war with the Indians in order to weaken the citizen militia of Virginia. Since Dunmore remained loyal to the British during the American Revolution, Poffenbarger argued that Dunmore incited the battle to give the British an advantage in any future conflict with the colonies. Poffenbarger even referred to Dunmore as the "Tory Governor" of Virginia.[42] To support her theory, Poffenbarger cited the fact that Dunmore's Northern Division never joined with Lewis' Southern Division. She argued that this was a deliberate act by Dunmore in order to leave Lewis and his men open for annihilation. Poffenbarger noted that the day before the Battle of Point Pleasant, a Shawnee Chief named Blue Jacket visited with Dunmore and continued directly to Point Pleasant thereafter,[43] thereby suggesting that the

---

[42] Livia Simpson-Poffenbarger, Point Pleasant, Mason County West Virginia Original Information Web Site, "The Battle of Point Pleasant: First Battle of the American Revolution October 10, 1774," http://www.pointpleasantwv.org/Parks&Campgrounds/StateParks/TuEndiWei/TuEndieWei-Hello.htm (accessed December 31, 2007).

Indians collaborated with Dunmore. Historian John P. Hale supported the idea that Dunmore sought to sabotage the militia when he wrote, "it has been stated that there were not only suspicious but grave charges that Governor Dunmore acted a double part, and that he was untrue and treacherous to the interests of the colony he governed.[44] Poffenbarger further noted that General Lewis was aware of Dunmore's treachery shortly following the battle, which explains why Lewis ignored orders to halt while he traveled north toward Dunmore immediately following the battle.[45] It also explains, according to Poffenbarger, why there exists no public record of the battle report made by General Lewis.[46]

It is further argued by Poffenbarger that at the time of the Battle of Point Pleasant the Indians were allied with

---

[43] Ibid.

[44] Ibid.

[45] Ibid.

[46] Ibid.

the British. This argument directly supports Poffenbarger's theory that the Battle of Point Pleasant was the first battle of the American Revolution. Poffenbarger noted that in the memoirs of Colonel John Stuart he wrote that "the Battle of Point Pleasant was in fact the beginning of the Revolutionary War . . . for it is well known that the Indians were influenced by the British to commence the war to terrify and confound the people."[47] Moreover, historian Virgil A. Lewis wrote that "Lord Dunmore was an enemy of the colonists, . . . hence his efforts to induce the Indians to cooperate with the English and thus reduce Virginia to subjection."[48] Poffenbarger also cites historian O.E. Randall who stated, "the Indians were the suborned subjects, the hired Hessians of the British, for whom and with whom they were eager to fight to defend the territory

---

[47] Ibid.

[48] Ibid.

reserved by the British for their hunting grounds and homes.[49]

Poffenbarger believed strongly that Lord Dunmore sought to weaken the Virginia militia and she maintained her conviction that the Indians colluded with Dunmore and were allied with the British. Poffenbarger rallied support for her theory until, in October 1901, the federal government dedicated a memorial park in memory of the Battle of Point Pleasant. The park, called Tu-Endie-Wei, marks the Battle of Point Pleasant as the first battle of the American Revolution.

Despite arguments that the Battle of Point Pleasant belonged to the American Revolution, evidence removes any connection the battle may have had with the Revolution. Primarily, Lord Dunmore held the interests of Virginia and its inhabitants to the highest regard and therefore never opposed the colony's best interests. First of

---

[49] Ibid.

all, Dunmore did not immediately support action taken against the Indians. In fact, Dunmore spoke against the House of Burgesses for authorizing him to prosecute war.[50] Instead it was General Andrew Lewis who "proposed that an adequate force be raised and marched to the frontier with the least possible delay."[51] Also, Dunmore was against actions taken by settlers which exacerbated frontier conflict. Dunmore spoke against the settler's habit of breaking treaties of which he wrote, "I by no means pretend to justify."[52] Regarding the Yellow Creek incident, Lord Dunmore sought diligently to punish those involved.[53]

---

[50] Lewis, *Battle of Point Pleasant*, 85.

[51] Hass, *History of the Early Settlement*, 150.

[52] Ibid., 371; Furthermore, in his official report, Dunmore pleaded that "I have invariably taken every step which depended on me, to prevent any infringement of . . . [the treaty of Fort Stanwix] by the people of this colony."; Thwaites, *Documentary History*, 370-371.

[53] Commenting on the Yellow Creek incident Dunmore declared, "I do assure your Lordship that the pacification, which I have since effected, has not made me relax, in the smallest degree, my diligence, in finding ways to come at them, and in bringing them to the punishment due to such enormity: and I have the satisfaction to acquaint your Lordship that I have hopes my endeavors for this purpose will not prove unsuccessful."; Thwaites, *Documentary History*, 378.

Conduct of the setters, however, created intense pressure among frontier forces to take action against the Indians of western Virginia. In a letter written to Colonel William Preston, Major Arthur Campbell professed, "I hope your known tenderness and humanity will excite you to make a vigorous effort to defend the inhabitants."[54]

Although Lord Dunmore was reluctant to prosecute war, he supplied the armies with ammunition and ventured with them to the frontier enduring all the same hardships at his own risk. Following the conflict, Lord Dunmore himself stated that the continual miseries of the frontier "determined me to go up into that part of the country, and to exert my own immediate endeavors on this important occasion."[55] From Dunmore's generous action in supplying the frontiersman, historian C.W. Butterfield

---

[54] Thwaites, *Documentary History*, 58.

[55] Ibid., 383.

commented that there is “no doubt” in Lord Dunmore’s sincerity “as to his acting in good faith toward Virginia.”[56]

The exertion of Lord Dunmore in the Indian conflict earned him complete and genuine gratitude from soldiers, citizens, and fellow political officials. Everyone involved was very pleased with Dunmore’s conduct toward the frontier struggle. The officers in the battle showed their appreciation to Lord Dunmore in a resolution dated November 5, 1774, in which it was stated that “we entertain the greatest respect for . . . Lord Dunmore . . . and who, we are confident underwent the great fatigue of this singular campaign from no other motive than the true interest of this country.”[57] Further praise was shown in a resolution adopted by the Virginia Convention on March 20, 1775, in which the “most cordial thanks” were presented to Lord

---

[56] Butterfield, *The Washington-Crawford Letters*, 90; Theodore Roosevelt wrote that “there is no reason whatever to suppose that he (Dunmore) was not doing his best for the Virginians: he deserved their gratitude.”; Roosevelt, *Winning of the West*, 230.

[57] Lewis, *Battle of Point Pleasant*, 86; see appendix D.

Dunmore "for his truly noble, wise, and spirited conduct . . . which at once evinces his Excellency's attention to the true interests of this Colony."[58] These and other statements completely exonerate Lord Dunmore from the accusation of treachery.[59]

The notion that the Indians were allied with the British at the time of the Battle of Point Pleasant is completely false. Although the Indians were allied with the British during the American Revolution, this did not occur until 1777. In July, 1776, several commissioners were appointed to meet with Indian Representatives at Fort Pitt.

---

[58] Ibid., 91; George Washington was among the members who voted for this resolution. See appendix D.

[59] Historian Wills De Hass exonerated Lord Dunmore when he wrote, "The charge of treasonable design so industriously made against Dunmore, although plausible in part, is not sustained by facts and circumstances." In a letter by Valentine Crawford written to George Washington June 8, 1774, he stated, "it is a happy circumstance for us that Lord Dunmore is so warm in our favor. This gives us great resolution to stand our ground, what few of us are left; though the country is very thin." Also, an address was given by Colonel Christian's Fincastle men who fought at Point Pleasant in which great praise is given to Lord Dunmore. For this address see appendix D; De Hass, *History of the Early Settlement*, 167; Butterfield, *The Washington-Crawford Letters*, 90.

It is recorded that, "the Indians who assembled at the treaty gave the strongest assurance that they would remain neutral in the conflict between the Colonies and the mother country."[60] This demonstrates that the Indians could not have been allied with the British prior to 1776. The unfortunate death of Chief Cornstalk also refutes the inclination that the Indians were allied with the British in 1774. In the spring of 1777, Chief Cornstalk was compelled to visit the garrison at Point Pleasant in order to preserve peace.[61] Cornstalk sought to warn American forces that his fellow tribes had considered fighting for the British cause. Cornstalk was detained and eventually killed. However, this shows that as late as the spring of 1777, the Indians had still not been allied with the British, and therefore could not have been fighting for the British at the Battle of Point Pleasant.

---

[60] Butterfield, *The Washington-Crawford Letters*, 60.

[61] Hass, *History of the Early Settlement*, 171-172.

There remains several details to show that the Battle of Point Pleasant was a colonial battle and not the first battle of the American Revolution. For instance, the men who fought at Point Pleasant were not granted a pension as Revolutionary soldiers.[62] Since they had not fought in the American Revolution, they did not receive the same benefits of those who had. The soldiers did, however, get paid for their efforts. Their salary was paid by Britain in an ordinance signed by King Henry of England.[63] Another important detail is the uniforms worn by the soldiers at Point Pleasant. Fallen soldier Charles Lewis was killed in battle while wearing the uniform of an English colonel because he was still loyal to the British government.[64] Also not to be overlooked is the fact that the U.S. Congress

---

[62] West Virginia History Center, "Manufactured History: Re-Fighting the Battle of Point Pleasant," http://www.wvculture.org/history/journal_wvh/wvh56-5.html (accessed November 6, 2004).

[63] Lewis, *Battle of Point Pleasant*, 74.

[64] "Manufactured History."

declared that, "the Revolutionary War in opposition to the encroachments of Great Britain on the Civil Rights of the American Colonies commenced April 19, 1775," six months following the Battle of Point Pleasant.[65]

Because of its approximation to the American Revolution, the Battle of Point Pleasant has often been directly connected as a part of that struggle. Despite arguments of those who believe the Battle of Point Pleasant was the first battle of the American Revolution, this cannot be true. Foremost, the Battle of Point Pleasant, as defined by historian Reuben Gold Thwaites, "was the culmination of a long series of mutual grievances and outrages between the frontiersman of Virginia . . . and the savages of the Ohio Valley."[66] It was preceded by a generation of conflict in which compromise could not be negotiated and therefore ended in a bloody battle. The motives surrounding the

---

[65] Ibid.

[66] Thwaites, *Documentary History*, i.

Battle of Point Pleasant were completely separate from those which instigated the Revolution. Furthermore, accusations of treason toward Lord Dunmore, the governor of colonial Virginia, are wholly untrue. Lord Dunmore risked himself for the best interests of Virginia and he was paid nothing but gratitude for his genuine effort. Lastly, the Shawnee Indians could not have been allied with the British at the time of the battle. It was not until three years later that the Indians of the western frontier supported the British cause. Instead, it was a battle fought solely between colonial settlers and western Indians for rights to the frontier lands.

No matter how the Battle of Point Pleasant is classified it was indeed a significant event in United States history. Its victory resulted in two major consequences. Firstly, it allowed colonial forces to be free to use all resources against the British. Secondly, it opened the west to further settlement and eventual expansion across the entire continent. Theodore Roosevelt properly summarized the results of victory when he wrote, "it kept the Northwestern tribes quiet for the first two years of the Revolutionary struggle; and above all it rendered possible the settlement of Kentucky, and therefore the winning of the West."[67] In the same manner, historian Virgil Lewis referred to the men who fought at Point Pleasant as "empire builders."[68] The Battle of Point Pleasant ended the great colonial stage of American history thereby allowing independence to be sought and a nation to be born.

---

[67] Roosevelt, *The Winning of the West*, 291.

[68] Lewis, *Battle of Point Pleasant*, 69.

Appendix A: Letters

William Crawford to John Penn

April 8, 1774

Sir: - As some very extraordinary occurrences have lately happened in this county, it is necessary to write an account of them to you. That which I now give, is at the request and with the approbation of all the magistrates that are at present attending the court. A few weeks ago Mr. Connolly went to Stanton and was sworn in as a justice of the peace for Augusta county, in which it is pretended that the country about Pittsburgh is included. He had, before this, brought with him, from Williamsburg, commissions of the peace for several gentlemen in this part of the province, but none of them, I believe, have been accepted. A number of new militia officers have been lately appointed by Lord Dunmore; several musters of the militia have been held, and much confusion has been occasioned by them.

I am informed that the militia is composed of men without character and without fortune, and who would be equally averse to the regular administration of justice under the colony of Virginia as they are to that under the province of Pennsylvania. The disturbances which they have produced at Pittsburgh, have been continually alarming to the inhabitants. Mr. Connolly is constantly surrounded with a body of armed men. He boasts the countenance of the Governor of Virginia, and forcibly obstructs the execution of legal process, whether from the court or from single magistrates. A deputy sheriff has come from Augusta county, and I am told has writs in his hands against Captain St. Clair and the sheriff, for the arrest and confinement of Mr. Connolly.

The sheriff was last week arrested at Pittsburgh for serving a writ on one of the inhabitants there, but was, after some time, discharged. On Monday last, one of Connolly's people grossly insulted Mr. McKay, and was confined by him in order to be sent to jail; the rest of the party hearing of it, immediately came to Mr. McKay's house and proceeded to the most violent outrages. Mrs. McKay was wounded in the arm with a cutlass; the magistrates, and those who came to their assistance, were treated with much abuse, and the prisoner was rescued.

Some days before the meeting of the court, a report was spread that the militia of officers at the head of their several companies would come to Mr. Hanna's, use the Court ill, and interrupt the administration of justice. On Wednesday, while the Court was adjourned, they came to the courthouse and paraded before it; sentinels were placed at the door, and Mr. Connolly went into the house. One of the magistrates was hindered, by the militia, from going into it till permission was first obtained from their commander. Mr. Connolly sent a message to the magistrates, informing them that he wanted to communicate something to them, and would wait on them for that purpose.

They received him in a private room. He read to them the enclosed paper, together with a copy of a letter to you, which Lord Dunmore had transmitted to him, enclosed in a letter to himself, which was written in the same angry and undignified style. The magistrates gave the enclosed answer to what he read; and he soon afterwards departed with his men. Their number was about one hundred and eighty or two hundred. On their return to Pittsburgh, some of them seized Mr. Elliott, of the Bullock Pen, and threatened to put him in the stocks for something which they deemed an affront offered to their commander. Since their return, a certain Edward Thompson and a young man, would not allow him time even to look up the store. In other parts of the county, particularly those adjoining the river Monongahela; the magistrates have been frequently insulted in the most indecent and violent manner, and are apprehensive that, unless they are speedily and vigorously supported by the Government, it will become both fruitless and dangerous for them to proceed in the execution of their offices. They presume not to point out the measures proper for settling the present disturbances, but beg leave to recommend the fixing a temporary line with the utmost expedition, as one step, which, in all probability, will contribute very much toward producing that effect.

For further particulars concerning the situation of this country, I refer you to Colonel Wilson, who is kind enough to go on the present occasion to Philadelphia. I am, etc.[69]

William Crawford to George Washington

May 8, 1774

Sir: - Enclosed you have the drafts of the Round Bottom and your Chartier's land, finished agreeable to Mr. Lewis's direction. I should have sent them from Stanton, but Mr. Lewis had set out for Cheat river before I got there, and I wanted him to see the returns before I sent them to you. I was still disappointed, as before I could return back again Mr. Lewis started for home, and I understand he will be in Williamsburgh soon. If the returns do not answer, you can have them changed. If you should not choose to enter those names in the return now made for the Round

---

[69] C.W. Butterfield, ed., *The Washington-Crawford Letters: Being the Correspondence Between George Washington and William Crawford, from 1767-1781 Concerning Western Lands* (Cincinnati: Robert Clarke & Co., 1877), 42-46.

Bottom, I have sent you a blank to fill up, which you may do yourself.

I suppose by this time various reports have reached you. I have given myself some trouble to acquaint myself with the truth of matters; but there are some doubts remaining as to certain facts; however, I will give you the best account I can.

The surveyors that went down the Kanawha, as report goes, were stopped by the Shawanese Indians, upon which some of the white people attacked some Indians and killed several, took thirty horse-loads of skins near the mouth of Scioto; on which news, and expecting an Indian war, Mr. Cresap and some other people fell on some other Indians at the mouth of Pipe creek, killed three, and scalped them. Daniel Greathouse and some others fell on some at the mouth of Yellow creek and killed and scalped ten, and took one child about two months old, which is now at my house. I have taken the child from a woman that it had been given to. Our inhabitants are much alarmed, many hundreds having gone over the mountain, and the whole country evacuated as far as the Monongahela; and many on this side of the river are gone over the mountain. In short, a war is every moment expected. We have a council now with the Indians. What will be the event I do not know.

I am now setting out for Fort Pitt at the head of one hundred men. Many others are to meet me there and at Wheeling, where we shall wait the motions of the Indians and shall act accordingly. We are in great want of some proper person to direct us, who may have command, - Mr. Connolly, who now commands, having incurred the displeasure of the people. He is unable to take command for two reasons: one is, the contradiction between us and the Pennsylvanians; and the other that he carries matters too much in a military way, and is not able to go through with it. I have some hopes that we may still have matters settled with the Indians upon a method properly adopted for that purpose.

It seems that they say they have not been paid anything for their land – I mean the Shawanese and Delawares. The Six Nations say they have no right to any of the money, the land not being their property. I do not mean to say anything against Mr. Connolly's conduct, only he can not carry things on as he could wish, as he is not well acquainted with the nature of the people he has to deal with. Fair means would do better, and he could get anything he wanted more readily.

In case of a war, much dependence from this place lies on you, Sir, as being well acquainted with our circumstances. Should matters be settled with the Indians soon, I suppose you will proceed on with the improvement of your lands; if not, you will discharge your people, and of course your servants will be sold. In that case, I should be glad to take two of them, if you are willing. In a few days you will be better advised, and then you will be more able to determine on matters. I am, &c.[70]

William Crawford to George Washington

June 8, 1774

Dear Sir: - I received your letter by Mr. Christy dated 27th of May; and I am sorry you seem to be in confusion as well as us, as that renders our case more deplorable. Saturday last we had six persons killed on Dunkard's creek, about ten miles from the mouth of Cheat river on the west side of Monongahela, and there are three missing. On Sunday, a man who left a party is supposed to be killed, as he went off to hunt some horses, and five guns

---

[70] Ibid., 46-50.

were heard go off. The horse he rode away returned to the house where the party was. They set out in search of enemies; found the man's coat, and saw a number of tracks, but could not find the man. Our whole country is in forts, what is left; but the major part is gone over the mountain. With much ado I have prevailed on about a dozen of families to join me in building a fort over against my house, which has been accomplished with much difficulty and a considerable expense to me. Valentine Crawford has built another at the same rate.

It was with great difficulty any could be prevailed upon to stay, such was the panic that seized the people. If something is not done, I am much afraid the whole country must fall into the hands of the enemy. The Delawares seem to be on our side as yet; but on them there is not much dependence. I believe an Indian war is unavoidable. I have been on a scouting party as low as Grave creek since Mr. Johnston went down to Williamsburg, but could see no signs of any parties. However, as soon as I returned, a party crossed the river that did that mischief. Fort Pitt is blockaded, and the inhabitants of the town are about picketing it in. They have about one hundred men fit for arms in town and fort, which I do not think sufficient to protect those places.

I shall take the opportunity of the first scouting party down the river to comply with your request in regard to the Round Bottom, and send you a plat and another to Mr. Lewis. Then I hope no door will be left open for disappointment. As to the variation of the compass, it has been taken by Mr. Leet and Mr. McLain from Mr. Dixon and Mason's calculations; and they find it to be 4°10' westerly. Their work, I believe, may be depended upon, as they are both able surveyors.

I am at a loss what to advise you or Valentine Crawford to do in regard to your people. At times I am afraid they will be very troublesome. I am afraid, should that be the case, little would be done for your advantage. In your letter to Valentine Crawford, you wrote about a mistake in laying a new county. I apprehended by Lord Dunmore, there was a new county intended on the west of the mountain. I am, etc.

P.S. – We are in great want of guns and ammunition.[71]

Major Arthur Campbell to Colonel William Preston

Dear Sir – The hour that I so much dreaded (as to the peace of this country) is now I am apprehensive near at hand; the Cherokees has at length commenced hostilities.

The[y] have murdered their Traders, and the Messengers that went from Wattago and I expect the principal part of this country will meet with the same fate soon, if not speedily succored, there is forty Shawanese in the Cherokee towns I hope your known tenderness and humanity will excite you to make a vigorous effort to defend the Inhabitants; I am certain the[y] will all below Stalnacres fly before the enemy; as the scarcity of ammunition is the general cry. I hope the Pittsylvania and Bedford Militia will be drawn out on this occasion. For could we be able to face them about the lower settlement on this river the war might not be so calamitous. In consequence of your former orders I have requested of Capt. Crockett and Doack one half of their men to meet against next Tuesday or sooner at the town house. You can direct matters down lower as may be best.

I am Sir Your most Obedient

Arthur Campbell

July 1st, 1774[72]

---

[71] Ibid., 50-52.

Extract from a letter of Col. William Preston to George Washington

Smithfield, August 15, 1774:

Mr. Thomas Hog who brought the plats of your land on Cole River from Capt. Floyd in April last with two other men has never since been heard of, so that there is no doubt of their being killed or taken, but I fear the former is the case. Capt. Floyd with three others came in last Saturday; the other surveyors with a party of men are still out, but there is some reason to hope they are safe.

We are greatly harassed by the enemy in this country: About ten days ago, a small party killed five persons, mostly children, and took three prisoners about fifteen miles from this place, which is greatly exposed. I began yesterday to build a fort about my house for the defense of my family.[73]

---

[72] Reuben Gold Thwaites and Louise Phelps Kellogg, eds., *Documentary History of Dunmore's War, 1774* (Madison, WI: Wisconsin Historical Society, 1905), 57-58.

[73] Ibid. 151.

Appendix B: Personal Accounts

Account of McDonald's Expedition from Dr. Draper

Early in June Dunmore planned an expedition against the Indian towns, but it was not until July that McDonald succeeded in securing a force sufficient to move out. About 400 were then recruited, chiefly on the Monongahela and Youghiogheny, under the following captains: Michael Cresap, Michael Cresap, Jr. (nephew of the preceding), Hancock Lee, Daniel Morgan, James Wood, Henry Hoagland, and probably two others. Marching across country and joining Crawford at Wheeling, where he was left in command of Fort Fincastle, McDonald ordered every man to take seven days' provisions in his pack, and crossed the river (July 26) at the mouth of Fish Creek, some twenty-four miles below Wheeling, whither they had floated down in canoes. George Rogers Clark, who had a land-claim in this vicinity, was a subaltern in Cresap's command. From the point of crossing, the towns were about ninety miles distant. No enemy was seen until within six miles of Wakatomica, where about thirty Indians awaited the columns, in ambush at the head of a swampy crossing. A slight skirmish of thirty minutes resulted in the killing of four Indians and wounding others, when the enemy broke and fled. The whites lost two killed and five wounded, among the former a frontiersman named Martin; among the latter Nathaniel Fox, William Linn, and John Hardin. Leaving a small party to care for the wounded, the army pushed on to the Muskingum, where they arrived about nightfall of the second of August. The Indians were posted on the opposite bank, prepared to dispute the passage, and protect the first town. After some sharp-shooting, darkness put an end to the combat, and the whites withdrew to hold a council of war on the expediency of forcing passage across the stream. Cresap's and Hoagland's companies were detached to deploy some miles below, and at the break of day cross and make a flank movement on the towns. Meanwhile an interpreter brought in a Delaware and Mingo, who requested peace. The former was told that strict orders had been issued to molest no friendly Indians, the latter was sent to bring hostages from the Shawnee. He returned later unsuccessful, and was the prisoner brought back by the expedition. Cresap spent the night in preparation, and moved out two hours before dawn, crossed the river, and had a slight skirmish in which the leader himself killed one Indian, and others were wounded. The towns were found abandoned. After burning five villages, and cutting down seventy acres of standing corn, the army, then almost entirely destitute of provisions, crossed country to Wheeling. A small party of Pennsylvanians, led by Devereux Smith, and of Delaware Indians under White Eyes, had come to Wheeling two days after the army had started on their out-going march. Crawford discouraged their attempting to overtake the expedition, whereupon they returned to Pittsburg. The results of the expedition were slight, ravages upon the frontiers thereafter increasing rather than diminishing. But the body of men who had been enlisted, awaited at Redstone the Wing of the army taken out by Lord Dunmore. – Ed.[74]

Isaac Shelby's Account of the Battle

---

[74] Thwaites, *Documentary History*, 154-156.

October 16, 1774

On Monday morning, about half an hour before sun-rise, two of Captains Russell's Company discovered a large party of Indians about a mile from camp, one of which men was shot down by the Indians, the other made his escape and brought the intelligence. In two or three minutes after, two of Captain Shelby's came in and confirmed the account. General Andrew Lewis being informed thereof, immediately ordered out Colonel Charles Lewis to take the command of one hundred and fifty of the Augusta Troops, and with him went Captain Dickinson, Captain Harrison, Captain Wilson, Captain John Lewis, of Augusta, and Captain Lockridge, which made the first Division. Colonel Fleming was also ordered to take the command of one hundred and fifty more of the Botetourt, Bedford, and Fincastle Troops, viz: Captain Thomas Buford, from Bedford, Captain Love, of Botetourt, Captain Shelby and Captain Russell, of Fincastle, which made the second Division. Colonel Charles Lewis's Division marched to the right some distance from the Ohio; and Colonel Fleming, with his Division, on the bank of the Ohio, to the left. Colonel Charles Lewis's Division had not marched quite half a mile from camp, when, about sun-rise, an attack was made on the front of his Division, in a most vigorous manner, by untied tribes of Indians, Shawnees, Delawares, Mingoes, Tawas, (Ottawas) and of several other nations, in number not less than eight hundred, and by many thought to be a thousand. In this heavy attack, Colonel Charles Lewis received a wound, which in a few hours caused his death, and several of his men fell on the spot. In fact, the Augusta Division was forced to give way to the heavy fire of the enemy. In about a second of a minute after the attack on Colonel Lewis's Division, the enemy engaged the front of Colonel Fleming's Division, on the Ohio and in a short time the Colonel received two balls through his left arm, and one through his breast and after animating the officers and soldiers in a most calm manner, to the pursuit of victory, retired to the camp. This loss from the field was sensibly felt by the officers in particular; but the Augusta Troops being shortly reinforced from the camp by Colonel Field, with his Company, together with Captain McDowell, Captain Matthews, and Captain Stuart, from Augusta, Captain John Lewis, Captain Pauling, Captain Arbuckle, and Captain McClennahan, from Boteourt, the enemy, no longer able to maintain their ground, was forced to give way till they were in a line with the troops, which Colonel Fleming had left in action on the bank of the Ohio. In this precipitate retreat, Colonel Field was killed. During this time, which was till after twelve o'clock, the action continued extremely hot. The close underwood, many steep banks and logs, greatly favored their retreat; and the bravest of their men made the best use of them whilst others were throwing their dead into the Ohio, and carrying off their wounded. After twelve, the action in a small degree abated, but continued, except at short intervals, sharp enough till after one o'clock. Their long retreat gave them a most advantageous spot of ground, from whence it appeared to the officers so difficult to dislodge them, that it was thought most advisable to stand, as the line was then formed, which was about a mile and a quarter in length, and had sustained till then a constant and equal weight of the action, from wing to wing. It was till about half an hour of sunset they continued firing on us scattering shots, which we retuned to their disadvantage. At length night coming on, they found a safe retreat. They had not the satisfaction of carrying off any of our men's scalps, save one or two stragglers, whom they killed before the engagement. Many of their dead they scalped, rather than we should have them; but our troops scalped upwards of twenty of their men that were first killed. It is beyond doubt their loss in number, far exceeds ours, which is considerable.[75]

[75] Virgil A. Lewis, *History of the Battle of Point Pleasant* (Charleston, WV: The Tribune Printing Company, 1909), 43-45.

Appendix C: Agreements

Proclamation, by Henry Bouquet, Esquire, Colonel of Foot, and Commanding at Fort Pitt and Dependencies.

"Whereas, by a treaty at Easton, in the year 1758, and afterwards ratified by his Majesty's ministers, the country to the west of the Alleghany mountain is allowed to the Indians for their hunting ground. And as it is of the highest importance to his Majesty's service, and the preservation of the peace, and a good understanding with the Indians, to avoid giving them any just cause of complaint: this is therefore to forbid any of his Majesty's subjects to settle or hunt to the west of the Alleghany mountains, on any pretence whatever, unless such have obtained leave in writing from the general, or the governors of their respective provinces, and produce the same to the commanding officer at Fort Pitt. And all the officers and non-commissioned officers, commanding at the several posts erected in that part of the country, for the protection of the trade, are hereby ordered to seize, or cause to be seized, any of his Majesty's subjects, who, without the above authority, should pretend, after the publication hereof, to settle or hunt upon the said lands, and send them, with their horses and effects, to Fort Pitt, there to be tried and punished according to the nature of their offence, by the sentence of a court material.

Henry Bouquet."[76]

---

[76] Wills De Hass, *History of the Early Settlement and Indian Wars of Western Virginia* (Wheeling, WV: H.Hoblitzell, 1851), 131-132.

Treaty of Camp Charlotte
The Terms of Our Reconciliation

I. To give up, without reserve all the prisoners ever taken by them in war with the white people; and to never again wage war against the frontier of Virginia.

II. To give up all negroes taken by them from white people since the last war; and to pay for all property destroyed by them in that time.

III. To surrender all horses and other valuable effects which they had taken from the white people since the last war.

IV. To no more in the future hunt on or visit the south side of the Ohio river, except for the purpose of trading with the white people.

V. To no more molest boats of white people, while descending or ascending the Ohio river.

VI. To agree to such regulations for trade with the white people as should hereafter be dictated by the King's instruction.

VII. To deliver up hostages as a guarantee for the faithful compliance with the terms of the treaty; to be kept by the Whites until convinced of the sincerity on the part of the Indians to adhere to all these articles.

VIII. To have from the Governor a guarantee that no white people should be permitted to hunt on the northern, or Indian side of the Ohio river.

IX. To meet at Pittsburg the next spring and enter into a supplemental treaty by which the terms of the treaty of "Camp Charlotte" should be ratified and fully confirmed.[77]

[77] Lewis, *Battle of Point Pleasant*, 56.

Appendix D: Gratitude Paid to Lord Dunmore

A Resolution by the Officers, Who Served Under Lord Dunmore, Adopted at Fort Gower, Mouth of the Hockhocking River, November 5, 1774.

"Resolved, that we entertain the greatest respect for his Excellency the Right Honorable Lord Dunmore, who commanded the expedition against the Shawanese; and who, we are confident underwent the great fatigue of this singular campaign from no other motive than the true interest of this country.

Signed by order and in behalf of the whole Corps,

Benjamin Ashby, Clerk."[78]

Resolution Adopted by the Virginia Convention Which Assembled at Richmond, March 20, 1775.

"Resolved Unanimously, that the most cordial thanks of the people of this Colony are a tribute justly due to our worthy Governor, Lord Dunmore, for his truly noble, wise, and spirited conduct on the late expedition against our Indian enemy; a conduct which at once evinces his Excellency's attention to the true interest of this Colony, and a zeal in the Executive Department which no dangers can divert or difficulties hinder from achieving the most important services to the people who have the happiness to live under his administration."[79]

---

[78] Lewis, *Battle of Point Pleasant*, 86.

[79] Ibid., 91.

Address of Freeholders of Fincastle County (Virginia) to Lord Dunmore, April 8, 1775.

To his Excellency the Right Honorable John, Earl of Dunmore, His Majesty's Lieutenant and Governor-General of the Colony of Virginia:

"My Lord: - Notwithstanding the unhappy disputes that a present subsist between the Mother Country and the Colonies, in which we have given the public our sentiments, yet justice and gratitude, as well as a sense of our duty, induce us collectively to return your Lordship our unfeigned thanks for the great services you have rendered the frontiers in general, and this county in particular, in the late expedition against our enemy Indians.

In our former wars with the savages, we long suffered every species of barbarity; many of our friends and fellow-subjects were inhumanly butchered and carried into captivity, more to be dreaded than death itself; our houses plundered and burned and our country laid waste by an enemy, against whom, form our dispersed situation, and their manner of carrying on war, it was impossible to make a proper defense on our frontiers. Your Lordship being convinced of this, proposed to attack the enemy in their own country, well judging that it would be the most effectual means to reduce them to reason, and be attended with little more expense to the community than a partial defense of such an extensive frontier. The proposal was cheerfully embraced, and the ardor of the militia to engage in that very necessary service, could only be equaled by that of your Lordship in carrying it on. That the plan of an expedition should be laid when the season was far advanced, and near three thousand choice troops raised in a few counties, and put under the command of many brave and experienced officers; that those forces should be equipped and fully supplied with provisions, and march several hundred miles through mountains to meet the enemy; that so many nations of warlike Indians should be reduced to sue for peace; that those troops should return victorious to their homes by the last of November; and all this without any public money in hand to defray any part of the expense, shows at first view the immediate utility of the undertaking, and must be a convincing proof that the Almighty, in a peculiar manner, blessed our Lordship's attempts to establish peace, and stop the further effusion of human blood; but that your Lordship should forego your ease, and every domestic felicity, and march at the head of a body of those troops many hundred miles from the seat of government, cheerfully undergoing all the fatigues of the campaign, by exposing your person, and marching on foot with the officers and soldiers, commands our warmest returns of gratitude; and the rather, as we have no instance of such condescension in your Lordship's predecessors on any similar occasion.

We should be wanting in point of gratitude, were we to omit retuning our thanks on this occasion to the officers and soldiers who entered into the service with so much alacrity. The memory of such as feel nobly fighting for their country ought to be very dear to it.

That your Lordship may enjoy every domestic blessing; that you may long govern the brave and free people of Virginia, and that the present disturbances may be amicably settled, is the ardent wish of the inhabitants of Fincastle."[80]

---

[80] Ibid., 92-93.

Bibliography

Books

Butterfield, C.W., ed. The Washington-Crawford Letters: Being the Correspondence Between George Washington and William Crawford, from 1767 to 1781, Concerning Western Lands. Cincinnati: Robert Clarke & Co., 1877.

De Hass, Wills. History of the Early Settlement and Indians Wars of Western Virginia. Wheeling, WV: H. Hoblitzell, 1851.

Drake, Samuel G. Biography and History of the Indians of North America from its First Discovery. 11th ed. Boston: Benjamin B. Mussey and Co., 1851.

Roosevelt, Theodore, The Works of Theodore Roosevelt. Vol. 1, The Winning of the West. St. Claire Shores, MI: Scholarly Press, 1977, 1900.

Thwaites, Reuben Gold, and Louise Phelps Kellogg., eds. Documentary History of Dunmore's War. Madison, WI: Wisconsin Historical Society, 1905.

Online Material

Simpson-Poffenbarger, Livia. Point Pleasant, Mason County West Virginia Original Information Web Site. "The Battle of Point Pleasant: First Battle of the American Revolution October 10, 1774." http://www.pointpleasantwv.org/Parks&Campgrounds/StateParks/TuEndiWei/TuEndieWei-Hello.htm.

West Virginia History Center, “Manufactured History: Re-Fighting the Battle of Point Pleasant,” http://www.wvculture.org/history/journal_wvh/wvh56-5.html (accessed November 6, 2004).

www.ingramcontent.com/pod-product-compliance
Ingram Content Group UK Ltd.
Pitfield, Milton Keynes, MK11 3LW, UK
UKHW041838200726
13854UKWH00003BA/1206